BOMBUS
The Bumblebee

Elsie Larson

Illustrated by David Haidle

and Elizabeth Haidle

Master
Books

BOMBUS, THE BUMBLEBEE
First Printing: February 1997

© 1997 Elsie Larson
Illustrations © David & Elizabeth Haidle

ISBN: 0-89051-177-2

God's Blessings to the Students at Fairview Elementary

DEDICATIONS

With thanks and much affection
to my long-time friend Patricia Jane Hershiser,
who always encourages me to "take-off and fly."
— E. L.

To the other three in our family beehive:
Helen, Jonathan, and Paul.
Without their unsolicited opinions
this book would have been easier, but not as good.
— D. H. & E. H.

A Gift from the [...] and Emma Schrock

God spoke and there was earth and sea and sky.

God spoke again and created all kinds of animals, birds, fish, and insects. Each creature, great or small, was different from any other one.

God watched them all — swimming, swooping, leaping, creeping, and flying — and said, "Very good!"

Bombus, one of the bumblebees God created, bobbed among the flowers of the new earth. Like the honeybees, he drank nectar for breakfast, lunch, supper, and snacks. Unlike the honeybees, however, he could barely squeeze his big, fat body into some of the blossoms.

Bombus was big, and he was noisy. Other bees buzzed. The bumblebee rumbled. Also, he was clumsy. While the honeybees darted in straight flight, he lurched from side to side, bumping stems and leaves.

The honeybees soon discovered that Bombus Bumblebee did not leave much nectar for them. Although they raced to be first to a flower, Bombus usually won. When he bumbled into their flight path, they could only turn away or let him crash into them.

Once Bombus spied the best blossom,
the honeybees took second best.
Or so they thought.

Finally the small bees decided on a plan to trick
Bombus. Early one morning they waited for him by the
tallest, sweetest flowers. When he arrived, they greeted
him politely.

"Good morning, Bombus," they buzzed.

"Good morning," he answered.

"We have all been wondering," said one honeybee, "how anyone as large as you could fly."

"Why, I fly just like you do," answered Bombus.

"Oh no you don't!" said the small bee. "Watch! Can you do this?"

The honeybee darted straight up, did a zigzag dance, and gently landed on its flower perch.

Bombus fanned his wings so fast they hummed like a honeybee's wings. He leaped straight up. Instead of flying, he wobbled to the left and then to the right. Losing control, down he plopped.

"Watch us," cried the other honeybees. Away they zipped. Bombus carefully watched each of their movements. They darted this way and that, up and down, performing intricate honeybee dances. Their striped bodies flew in perfect balance under long wings.

"Haven't you looked at yourself?" called one of the honeybees. "Your body is much too fat and heavy for your wings. You are not shaped right for flight."

Bombus looked at himself. His huge body was coated with thick fur. His wings were short.

Even his legs looked bulky and heavy compared to the small bees' legs. For the first time Bombus realized how different he was from other bees.

The honeybees settled around him in a circle. One of them said, "It is obvious you were not meant to be a flying insect."

Another bee said, "You must have misunderstood your instructions. You are not supposed to fly."

"You should crawl," the bees sang in their humming voices. "Crawl like an ant!"

"No!" Bombus cried. "I can fly!" His stubby wings shook with anger. He stumbled and tipped nose down on his flower.

The honeybees laughed and laughed.

Bombus couldn't say a word. Even though the fall had not hurt him, he felt a strange pain somewhere under his furry coat. He thought, *I am fat and ugly and different. No wonder I can't fly like they do.* The pain grew.

The honeybees left. They zoomed to the highest, most colorful blossoms.

As they gathered nectar, they gleefully hummed to each other, "No Bombus to bump us."

"No Bombus to rush us."

"No Bombus to gobble the best."

They had distracted the big bee from the finest feast of all.

Poor Bombus was more than distracted. He was flustered.

Sadly he watched flies dart, wasps hover, and mosquitoes flit.

They all fly. Why can't I? he wondered.

Bombus watched the dragonfly, butterfly, and moth. He could not drift in the air as they did. Could it be that God had not meant for him to fly?

"Oh," he said to himself, "if only I had listened more carefully in the beginning." For a long time he sat and thought. He tried to remember exactly what God had said.

Suddenly Bombus heard a loud roar. A giant beetle flew over. It beat the air with powerful wings. Its heavy body wobbled in flight. Bombus tingled with excitement. "He's big like me! Maybe I can fly slowly like he does." Bombus stretched, groomed his fur, and braced his feet. Still, Bombus worried. *I wonder how he takes off?*

Raising his wings, Bombus slowly flapped. He could not make them roar like the beetle's wings. He jumped into the air anyway. Ker-plop! He fell on his fat stomach.

The honeybees are right, he decided. *I was not created to fly. I will join the creeping things.* The thought made him feel heavier and heavier.

While the honeybees buzzed in effortess flight above him, Bombus crawled up and down the shortest plants in search of nectar. By evening he was so tired, he decided to sleep on the last zinnia blossom he had climbed.

Just as he tucked his aching feet into the top of the bloom, the voice of God called gently, "Bombus, what are you doing? Why are you climbing up and down the flowers?"

"Oh, Most High, I made a mistake!" Bombus bumbled. "I thought I could fly like the honeybees. Now I understand that I can't. I can only crawl like the ants and caterpillars."

"What made you think you cannot fly?" asked God.

"The honeybees showed me that I am not shaped right for flying," said Bombus.

"I shall speak to the honeybees," said God in a voice that shook the tops of the highest hollyhocks. "But you, Bombus, listen to me."

Bombus listened VERY carefully. God said, "I told you to fly. No matter what your shape or weight, you can fly because I gave you flight. Now, lift up your wings . . . and FLY."

Bombus forgot about the dancing honeybees. He thought only of the words of God. He lifted his wings. He fanned them to a steady rumble. And away he flew — not like a honeybee or dragonfly or beetle — but like a bumblebee.

From that day to this, bumblebees have always flown.
Even so, for thousands of years everyone said bumblebees
were not shaped right for flight. No one knew how their
short wings could lift their heavy bodies. No one knew
but God, who gave them the power to fly.

FUN FACTS...
about Bumblebees:

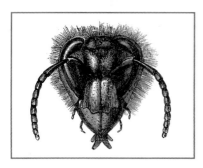

So how do bumblebees fly? Hold your arms out like airplane wings. Now try to move them by using only the muscles in your chest and back. Bumblebees do this nearly 200 times per second when they fly.

While your arms are straight out like wings, keep your elbows stiff and turn your hands, palms toward the floor and then toward the ceiling. If you were a bumblebee, you would be altering the pitch of your wings.

Changing the angle at which wings bite the air controls direction. A bumblebee does not whirl its wings like a helicopter, but lifts off and turns using the same process of altering the pitch of its wings.

To move its wings up and down, a bumblebee uses muscles inside the part of its body that compares to our rib cage (the bee's thorax). When these inner muscles contract, they change the shape of its thorax, much like a soft balloon changes shape if you flatten it with your hand and then let it swell again. Each time a bumblebee sucks in its thorax and lets go, its wings go up and down.

A bumblebee is warm-blooded. Its fur helps to keep it warm. It can fly only if its muscles are not too cool or too warm.

Only recently scientists have learned that a bumblebee controls its temperature, warming up before flight and avoiding overheating during flight. Also, it increases its strength by warming itself. If a load is too heavy, the bee shivers its thorax muscles to warm them.

A bumblebee uses sugar for fuel. During flight it uses twice as much fuel as would a hummingbird of equal weight. Ninety percent of its "tank full" of sugar goes to heat its muscles.

Bumblebees are worth tens of millions of dollars each year to farmers, because they are the only bees with long enough tongues to pollinate the deep blossoms of red clover. All worker bees are females. Males fly out in search of territory for a new young queen.

The scientific name for bumblebee is *Bombus*.

A Talking Time

Let questions flow into a two-way conversation, with the adult as well as the child telling some experiences that led to hurt feelings.

• Why did Bombus fall down and think he couldn't fly?
• Why did Bombus believe the honeybees?
• Has anyone ever said something that made you feel clumsy, ugly,
  or bad, because you are different?
  How did you feel?

• Have other children teased you, because you could not do what
  they could do, or because you didn't look like them?
  What did you do? *(Discuss being too **quick** to give up and the fact
  that some skills take much time, effort, and practice to learn).*
  What could you say or do, if you are teased again?

• Have you ever acted like the honeybees?
  What happened?
  What is a better way?

• Why should you not compare yourself to others? *(Discuss the
  importance of self-acceptance and of accepting others.)*

• If there is something you don't like about yourself that you can't
  change, how can you turn it into something useful and good?

• Why could Bombus fly again at the end of the story?
• Who took away Bombus' ability to fly — the honeybees or Bombus?
  *(Eleanor Roosevelt said, "No one can make me feel inferior
  without my consent." The honeybees couldn't hurt Bombus,
  unless they could get him to agree with them.)*

Creative Activities

Chosen to remind us that we are each unique and that to be different is special; to stimulate creativeness and confidence in trying new things.

 BALLOON BUMBLEBEES
> *— a reminder of how bumblebees fly.*
Blow oval or round balloons only to a soft round stage.
If desired, make eyes on one end and black stripes on the body with a felt-tipped pen.
Draw, color, and cut paper wings.
Tape the wings, one on each side of the balloon.
Press on the balloon between the wings (the bee's back) to see how Bombus moved his wings up and down.

 FINGERPRINT BEES
> *— to show how individual and unique we are.*
Press thumb to inked stamp pad.
Make a thumbprint on paper.
On the thumbprint draw eyes, wings, stripes, and legs.
Make more prints, using all five fingers.

Thumbprints make bumblebees.
Smaller fingers make honeybees or other insects.
Kids may want to make imaginary things, too.

 PLASTER CASTS

— *(of hands or feet) to show uniqueness of each person.*
Get plaster of Paris from a pharmacy. Mix and pour into paper plates. Just before it sets up, press hands or feet into the surface of it. When it hardens it can be decorated with acrylic paint or just left white. If you wish to hang it, remove the paper plate and attach a stick-on picture hanger.

 TRACING SHADOWS

— *gives a chance to talk about: "I am me, I don't have to be like anyone else."*

Profile of face:
Fasten paper to the wall.
Darken the room and shine a flashlight on the child to make a shadow on the paper.
With several children, they can take turns holding the light and outlining each other's shadows.
The profiles may be blackened as silhouettes, or details may be drawn in and colored.
Shadow of whole body:
Trace on poster board, cut out, and dress in child's clothing.

 LOOK FOR BUMBLEBEE STICKERS:

Use to remind children that they can do and be whatever they were meant to be. Let children give them to friends who need to be encouraged.

 LEARN MORE ABOUT BEES:

Visit a library. Ask the librarian to help you find books that tell more about bumblebees.
Call a county extension office. Ask for names of local honeybee keepers. Ask one if you may visit to see how they tend bees.

 A SECRET SIGNAL:

Decide on a hand gesture to represent the flight of a bumblebee, and let it be a secret signal between you and your child to let her know she's doing great.

The wordless signal can be used in situations when you cannot speak because of distance or desire for privacy. If it helps, it may become a family tradition.

MORE IDEAS
from parents of confident kids:

In a case of hurt feelings, help a child to think about why the other person was cruel — what kind of unhappiness made the other person act mean? Why do we compare, "put down," or criticize?

Have a bedtime ritual of saying to each child, *"You are so special. We love you very much."*

Help a child realize that a disfigurement or disability need not limit potential. They are a whole person of great value. Find information about others who are in similar situations and have gone on to live their lives to the fullest potential. God loves each of us for *who* we are and has a plan for each of our lives.

Talk with children about what to say and do the next time anyone teases, belittles, or tries to discourage them.